DELIVERANCE
The Good Shepherd's Matchless Power to Save

By: Bradley K. Graham   Illustrated By: Gretchen O'Neill

Deliverance
The Good Shepherd's Matchless Power to Save
All Rights Reserved.
Copyright © 2019 Bradley K Graham
v4.0

The opinions expressed in this manuscript are solely the opinions of the author and do not represent the opinions or thoughts of the publisher. The author has represented and warranted full ownership and/or legal right to publish all the materials in this book.

This book may not be reproduced, transmitted, or stored in whole or in part by any means, including graphic, electronic, or mechanical without the express written consent of the publisher except in the case of brief quotations embodied in critical articles and reviews.

High Country Storytellers Inc

Paperback ISBN: 978-0-578-21176-3
Hardback ISBN: 978-0-578-21177-0

Library of Congress Control Number: 2018963257

Illustrated by Gretchen O'Neill. All rights reserved - used with permission.

PRINTED IN THE UNITED STATES OF AMERICA

Acknowledgements

To my parents and siblings, thank you for the power of your examples in my life.
Growing up in our family home together was Heaven on Earth.

To my grandchildren, born and unborn, I wrote this for you.
Obey the commandments of God, but also find joy and happiness that comes from repentance,
for we are all partakers of this heavenly gift.

To my children Landon and Kelsey, Abby and Tyler, Gretchen
and Chris, Jacosa and Zack, Sunee, Dallan and Nettie Ann, the words of this poem came
directly out of my soul, and from my own experience. I know the "song of redeeming love" that
comes from finding ourselves clean and pure before the Lord.
As good as you are, you will not live without sin. Lay claim on the healing power of the Savior,
and we will be able to "see eye to eye."

To my darling Carolyn, who knows me better than anyone else on earth
but still sees me like Heaven sees me, thank you for your constant and unchanging love.
Because of the Atonement, someday I might be the man you see in me!

The shackles sing the captor's fate
He lies in anguish on the floor;
Bound in chains he now must wait
Locked behind a prison door.

The crushing, brutal weight of sin
Brings death and woe to crimson souls
When evil is invited in
Destroying all eternal goals.

The captive in his harrowed guilt
Lies wounded in the fatal chains;
Tormented by the life he's built
His garments have eternal stains.

Upon the brink of death he cries
Upward in the dark of night;
Pleading prayers into the skies
That he will not give up the fight.

Suddenly a shaft of Light
Cuts the darkness of the cell,
Painfully restoring sight
Revealing the repentance trail.

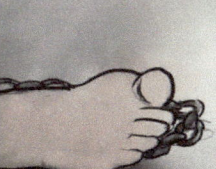

Wanting now to be alive
Working for another start.

Hidden hands and shoulders lift
Absorbing agonizing pain;
Burdens now begin to shift
Helping him to stand again.

Upon the path he sets his feet
Striving upward with his might;
Bitter memories turning sweet
On he goes toward the Light.

It doesn't happen suddenly
The marks of bondage disappear;
Realizing he is free
His conscience now is clean and clear.

Another life, another birth
The priceless gift from Mercy's throne!
He has more time while on the earth
To share the joy that he has known.

Instead of heavy, binding chains
Arms of love surround his soul.
He sings the beautiful refrains
Abounding from a heart that's full.

A pristine babe in Christ is born
And according to his faith is sealed;
And slowly he becomes aware
His inner wounds of sin are healed.

Deliverance
The Good Shepherd's Matchless Power to Save
By Bradley K Graham

The shackles sing the captor's fate
He lies in anguish on the floor;
Bound in chains he now must wait
Locked behind a prison door.

The crushing, brutal weight of sin
Brings death and woe to crimson souls
When evil is invited in
Destroying all eternal goals.

The captive in his harrowed guilt
Lies wounded in the fatal chains,
Tormented by the life he's built
His garments have eternal stains.

Upon the brink of death he cries
Upward in the dark of night:
Pleading prayers into the skies
That he will not give up the fight

Suddenly a shaft of Light
Cuts the darkness of the cell,
Painfully restoring sight
Revealing the repentance trail.

Faith and Hope again revive
Within his tender, broken heart;
Wanting now to be alive
Working for another start.

Hidden hands and shoulders lift
Absorbing agonizing pain;
Burdens now begin to shift
Helping him to stand again.

Upon the path he sets his feet
Striving upwards with his might.
Bitter memories turning sweet
On he goes towards the Light.

It doesn't happen suddenly
The marks of bondage disappear.
Realizing he is free
His conscience now is clean and clear.

Another life, another birth
A priceless gift from Mercy's throne!
He has more time while on the earth
To share the joy that he has known.

Instead of heavy, binding chains
Arms of love surround his soul;
He sings the beautiful refrains
Abounding from a heart that's full.

A pristine babe in Christ is born
And, according to his faith is sealed.
And slowly he becomes aware
His inner wounds of sin are healed.

Bradley Keith Graham grew up in rural Boise, Idaho, third of nine children in a home environment that could only be described as "Camelot". From an early age he memorized poems and stories that taught life lessons and values, following the teachings of Jesus of Nazareth as the framework for his life. As a student at BYU, and later as a missionary, he began to write stories and poems intended to lift, edify and teach the reader. In 1985 Brad married Carolyn Beales, the girl of his dreams and together they began building their own little kingdom of Camelot. Today, that kingdom includes their 7 children, along with 4 of their spouses and 9 grandkids who have joined the clan. These wonderful people, along with those that will surely come in the future, are the inspiration for all the stories and poems that come from Brad's pen. This book is Brad's second published work, and also the second collaborative effort with this daughter Gretchen, which is especially rewarding.

Gretchen Renee O'Neill was born in Cottonwood, Utah to Bradley and Carolyn Graham. Third of seven children Gretchen grew up in a home full of laughter and love. She was born with a gift, and as a little girl was always doodling, coloring or creating something beautiful to look at. As she grew older, she broadened her talent with study in oils, watercolor and even digital design. While earning her Art degree she met and married Christopher O'Neill, who shared her passion for life, as well as her eternal family goals. They have have been blessed with two beautiful children. Gretchen's ideas, thoughts and feelings are beautifully expressed in her art, and her illustrations in DELIVERANCE are deep with their own expressions of what Christ's Atonement means to her, and expand the meaning of the words exponentially.

If you like DELIVERANCE, please "like" us on Facebook at www.facebook.com/thedeliverancebook
Also, check out THE VOYAGE and "like" us at www.facebook.com/thevoyagebook
Visit our website at www.highcountrystorytellers.com for new titles coming soon!

STUDY GUIDE

Because DELIVERANCE is such a personal story, and because it deals with intimate and personal feelings, most who read it and associate with it's message will already have familiar scriptures and thoughts that quickly come to mind.
Because of it's spiritual overtones, and it's invitation to come unto Jesus Christ, we also felt to include a short study guide, certainly not comprehensive, but meant to assist those who want to learn more about the miracle of forgiveness the Savior offers.

Scriptures from several scriptural sources, include the King James Version of the Bible both Old and New Testament (KJV OT NT), The Book of Mormon, Another Testament of Jesus Christ (BOM), The Doctrine and Covenants (D&C), and Pearl of Great Price (POGP). While most are familiar with the King James Version of the Bible, some may not be familiar with the other books of scripture referenced here. A free and searchable copy of all sources above can be found at www.lds.org.

We hope these additional thoughts will point you to the Savior of the World, Jesus Christ, and his matchless love and power to save!

The shackles sing the captor's fate...

• *Acts 8:3* As for Saul, he made havoc of the church, entering into every house, and haling men and women committed them to prison. KJV NT

• *Acts 9: 1-9* And Saul, yet breathing out threatenings and slaughter against the disciples of the Lord, went unto the high priest, And desired of him letters to Damascus to the synagogues, that if he found any of this way, whether they were men or women, he might bring them bound unto Jerusalem. And as he journeyed, he came near Damascus: and suddenly there shined round about him a light from heaven: And he fell to the earth, and heard a voice saying unto him, **Saul, Saul, why persecutest thou me?** And he said, Who art thou, Lord? And the Lord said, I am Jesus whom thou persecutest: it is hard for thee to kick against the pricks. **And he trembling and astonished said, Lord, what wilt thou have me to do?** And the Lord said unto him, Arise, and go into the city, and it shall be told thee what thou must do. And the men which journeyed with him stood speechless, hearing a voice, but seeing no man. And Saul arose from the earth; and when his eyes were opened, he saw no man: but they led him by the hand, and brought him into Damascus. And he was three days without sight, and neither did eat nor drink. KJV NT

- *1 Peter 3:18-20* For Christ also hath once suffered for sins, the just for the unjust, that he might bring us to God, being put to death in the flesh, but quickened by the Spirit: By which also he went and preached unto the **spirits in prison**; Which sometime were disobedient, when once the longsuffering of God waited in the days of Noah, while the ark was a preparing, wherein few, that is, eight souls were saved by water. KJV NT

- *Alma 12:17* Then is the time when their torments shall be as a lake of fire and brimstone, whose flame ascendeth up forever and ever; and then is the time that they shall be chained down to an everlasting destruction, according to the power and captivity of Satan, he having subjected them according to his will. BOM

The crushing, brutal weight of sin...

- *2 Nephi 4:18* I am encompassed about, because of the temptations and the sins which do so easily beset me. BOM

- *Ephesians 5:6* Let no man deceive you with vain words: for because of these things cometh the wrath of God upon the children of disobedience. KJV NT

- *D&C 93:39* And that wicked one cometh and taketh away light and truth, through disobedience, from the children of men, and because of the tradition of their fathers. D&C

The captive in his harrowed guilt...

- *Alma 36:10-16* And it came to pass that I fell to the earth; and it was for the space of three days and three nights that I could not open my mouth, neither had I the use of my limbs. And the angel spake more things unto me, which were heard by my brethren, but I did not hear them; for when I heard the words—If thou wilt be destroyed of thyself, seek no more to destroy the church of God—I was struck with such great fear and amazement lest perhaps I should be destroyed, that I fell to the earth and I did hear no more. But I was racked with eternal torment, for my soul was harrowed up to the greatest degree and racked with all my sins. Yea, I did remember all my sins and iniquities, for which I was tormented with the pains of hell; yea, I saw that I had rebelled against my God, and that I had not kept his holy commandments. Yea, and I had murdered many of his children, or rather led them away unto destruction; yea, and in fine so great had been my iniquities, that the very thought of coming into the presence of my God did rack my soul with inexpressible horror. Oh, thought I, that I could be banished and become extinct both soul and body, that I might not be brought to stand in the presence of my God, to be judged of my deeds. And now, for three days and for three nights was I racked, even with the pains of a damned soul. BOM

- Alma 7:21 And he doth not dwell in unholy temples; neither can filthiness or anything which is unclean be received into the kingdom of God; therefore I say unto you the time shall come, yea, and it shall be at the last day, that he who is filthy shall remain in his filthiness. BOM

Upon the brink of death he cries…

- Psalms 107:19 Then they cry unto the Lord in their trouble, and he saveth them out of their distresses. KJV OT

- Isaiah 19:20 And it shall be for a sign and for a witness unto the Lord of hosts in the land of Egypt: for they shall cry unto the Lord because of the oppressors, and he shall send them a saviour, and a great one, and he shall deliver them. KJV OT

- Alma 36:17-18 And it came to pass that as I was thus racked with torment, while I was harrowed up by the memory of my many sins, behold, I remembered also to have heard my father prophesy unto the people concerning the coming of one Jesus Christ, a Son of God, to atone for the sins of the world. Now, as my mind caught hold upon this thought, I cried within my heart: O Jesus, thou Son of God, have mercy on me, who am in the gall of bitterness, and am encircled about by the everlasting chains of death. BOM

- Psalms 34:18 The Lord is nigh unto them that are of a broken heart; and saveth such as be of a contrite spirit. KJV OT

- Enos 1:4 And my soul hungered; and I kneeled down before my Maker, and I cried unto him in mighty prayer and supplication for mine own soul; and all the day long did I cry unto him; yea, and when the night came I did still raise my voice high that it reached the heavens. BOM

Suddenly, a shaft of light…

- Deuteronomy 31:8 And the Lord, he it is that doth go before thee; he will be with thee, he will not fail thee, neither forsake thee: fear not, neither be dismayed. KJV OT

- Ephesians 5:8 For ye were sometimes darkness, but now are ye light in the Lord: walk as children of light: KJV OT

- Matthew 4:16 The people which sat in darkness saw great light; and to them which sat in the region and shadow of death light is sprung up. KJV NT

- 1 John 1:5 This then is the message which we have heard of him, and declare unto you, that God is light, and in him is no darkness at all. KJV NT

- John 12:46 I am come a light into the world, that whosoever believeth on me should not abide in darkness. KJV NT

- Alma 36:20 And oh, what joy, and what marvelous light I did behold; yea, my soul was filled with joy as exceeding as was my pain! BOM

Faith and hope again revive...

- *Titus 2:13* Looking for that blessed hope, and the glorious appearing of the great God and our Saviour Jesus Christ; KJV NT

- *2 Corinthians 7:10* For godly sorrow worketh repentance to salvation not to be repented of: but the sorrow of the world worketh death. KJV NT

- *Mark 2:17* When Jesus heard it, he saith unto them, They that are whole have no need of the physician, but they that are sick: I came not to call the righteous, but sinners to repentance. KJV NT

- *Psalms 51:17* The sacrifices of God are a broken spirit: a broken and a contrite heart, O God, thou wilt not despise. KJV OT

- *3 Nephi 12:19* And behold, I have given you the law and the commandments of my Father, that ye shall believe in me, and that ye shall repent of your sins, and come unto me with a broken heart and a contrite spirit. Behold, ye have the commandments before you, and the law is fulfilled. BOM

- *Alma 22:18* O God, Aaron hath told me that there is a God; and if there is a God, and if thou art God, wilt thou make thyself known unto me, and I will give away all my sins to know thee, and that I may be raised from the dead, and be saved at the last day. And now when the king had said these words, he was struck as if he were dead. BOM

Hidden hands and shoulders lift...

- *Isaiah 53:4* Surely he hath borne our griefs, and carried our sorrows: yet we did esteem him stricken, smitten of God, and afflicted. KJV OT

- *3 Nephi 11:11* And behold, I am the light and the life of the world; and I have drunk out of that bitter cup which the Father hath given me, and have glorified the Father in taking upon me the sins of the world, in the which I have suffered the will of the Father in all things from the beginning. BOM

- *3 Nephi 11:14* Arise and come forth unto me, that ye may thrust your hands into my side, and also that ye may feel the prints of the nails in my hands and in my feet, that ye may know that I am the God of Israel, and the God of the whole earth, and have been slain for the sins of the world. BOM

- *Matthew 11:28* Come unto me, all ye that labour and are heavy laden, and I will give you rest. KJV NT

Upon the path he sets his feet...

• *Luke 15:7* 7 I say unto you, that likewise joy shall be in heaven over one sinner that repenteth, more than over ninety and nine just persons, which need no repentance. KJV NT

• *Alma 5:7* Behold, he changed their hearts; yea, he awakened them out of a deep sleep, and they awoke unto God. Behold, they were in the midst of darkness; nevertheless, their souls were illuminated by the light of the everlasting word; yea, they were encircled about by the bands of death, and the chains of hell, and an everlasting destruction did await them. BOM

• *Psalms 119:105* Thy word is a lamp unto my feet, and a light unto my path. KJV OT

• *Proverbs 4:26* Ponder the path of thy feet, and let all thy ways be established. KJV OT

• *Alma 36:21* Yea, I say unto you, my son, that there could be nothing so exquisite and so bitter as were my pains. Yea, and again I say unto you, my son, that on the other hand, there can be nothing so exquisite and sweet as was my joy. BOM

It doesn't happen suddenly...

• *Isaiah1:18* Come now, and let us reason together, saith the Lord: though your sins be as scarlet, they shall be as white as snow; though they be red like crimson, they shall be as wool. KJV OT

• *A Poor Wayfaring Man of Grief, Verse 5:* Stript, wounded, beaten nigh to death, I found him by the highway side. I roused his pulse, brought back his breath, Revived his spirit, and supplied Wine, oil, refreshment--he was healed. I had myself a wound concealed, But from that hour forgot the smart, And peace bound up my broken heart. JAMES MONTGOMERY, 1771-1854

• *Alma 26:14* Yea, we have reason to praise him forever, for he is the Most High God, and has loosed our brethren from the chains of hell. BOM

Another life, another birth...

• *John 3:3* Jesus answered and said unto him, Verily, verily, I say unto thee, Except a man be born again, he cannot see the kingdom of God. KJV NT

• *Mosiah 27:25-26* And the Lord said unto me: Marvel not that all mankind, yea, men and women, all nations, kindreds, tongues and people, must be born again; yea, born of God, changed from their carnal and fallen state, to a state of righteousness, being redeemed of God, becoming his sons and daughters; And thus they become new creatures; and unless they do this, they can in nowise inherit the kingdom of God. BOM

• *2 Corinthians 5:17* Therefore if any man be in Christ, he is a new creature: old things are passed away; behold, all things are become new. KJV NT

Instead of heavy, binding chains....

• *Alma 5:33* Behold, he sendeth an invitation unto all men, for the arms of mercy are extended towards them, and he saith: Repent, and I will receive you. BOM

• *2 Nephi 1:15* But behold, the Lord hath redeemed my soul from hell; I have beheld his glory, and I am encircled about eternally in the arms of his love. BOM

• *Psalms 59:16* But I will sing of thy power; yea, I will sing aloud of thy mercy in the morning: for thou hast been my defence and refuge in the day of my trouble. KJV OT

• *D&C 25:12* For my soul delighteth in the song of the heart; yea, the song of the righteous is a prayer unto me, and it shall be answered with a blessing upon their heads. D&C

• *Alma 5:26* And now behold, I say unto you, my brethren, if ye have experienced a change of heart, and if ye have felt to sing the song of redeeming love, I would ask, can ye feel so now? BOM

A pristine babe in Christ is born...

• *Titus 3:7* That being justified by his grace, we should be made heirs according to the hope of eternal life. KJV NT

• *Romans 6:4* Therefore we are buried with him by baptism into death: that like as Christ was raised up from the dead by the glory of the Father, even so we also should walk in newness of life. KJV NT

• *Romans 8:17* And if children, then heirs; heirs of God, and joint-heirs with Christ; if so be that we suffer with him, that we may be also glorified together. KJV NT

• *Moses 1:39* For behold, this is my work and my glory—to bring to pass the immortality and eternal life of man. POGP

• *Moroni 7:19* Wherefore, I beseech of you, brethren, that ye should search diligently in the light of Christ that ye may know good from evil; and if ye will lay hold upon every good thing, and condemn it not, ye certainly will be a child of Christ BOM

www.ingramcontent.com/pod-product-compliance
Lightning Source LLC
Chambersburg PA
CBHW041952150426
43198CB00005B/110